In our Liverpool 4

Cartoons by Bill Stott

CW00327739

It's 30 years since I came to live and work in the world's f
whilst Liverpool's changed a bit - in terms of posh flats overlooking the
Mersey, wheel clampers with portable phones and up-market pubs where
everybody drinks foreign lager from the bottle, the devastating Scouse
Humour remains as strong as ever

Bill Stott

Origination by: *Ian Boumphrey - Desk Top Publisher*

Published by: *Ian & Marilyn Boumphrey The Nook 7 Acrefield Road Prenton Wirral L42 8LD Tel/Fax 0151 608 7611*

Printed by: *Arroweline Hoylake L47 2BS*

ISBN   1-899241-10-8

Price
£2.99

"What's it like to stay at the Adelphi? Very boring actually - nobody swore, the food was brilliant and the manageress was all sweetness & light . . ."

"I'll have a bleeping huge steak, bleeping well done."

"Hello? Reception? There's a bloke with no clothes on across the road . . ."

*"The matress is £45 per night,
but you can have a bale of straw for a tenner . . ."*

"*Well, for £2,000 you can have a fortnight in Barbados, or an interesting weekend at the Adelphi.*"

"Apparently they've popped in to get staff's autographs . . ."

"If madam would care to delay her complaint -
the T.V. cameras will be here any minute."

"He hasn't got a kid at the school.
He just likes yelling at young people."

"Ooh luke - a Cuke!"

"And there's my very own teletubby . . ."

"Look at that - A Death Watch Beetle."

"Hey - that's really cool - drinking from a GLASS!"

"Our Terry was only six when we went in . . ."

"Aye Aye - it's Old Spice"

"Why do we wear our caps backwards?
If you have to ask the question, you won't understand the answer . . ."

"*Shame there are no tram lines for them to get stuck in . . .*"

"Why'd you pick it up grandad?"

"Looks like somebody's called for the silverware . . ."

"*Mam! Mam! Everton have scored again, gran's thrown her Horlicks at the telly, kicked the dog and said the 'F' word loads of times . . .*"

"Hello - Houston . . . Moscow?
We're being hailed by two blokes from Liverpool . . ."

THIS BAR IS BELOW STREET LEVEL. YOUR PHONE WONT WORK DOWN HERE, SO STOP TRYING TO IMPRESS PEOPLE

"Disruptive? Disobedient?
My goodness Mrs O'Hooligan - did I write this?"

"*Regulars just couldn't decide which new name to adopt.*"

"It's probably 'is mam telling 'im not to stand up there without a decent vest . . . !"

"The only underwater spoon-playing granny in Liverpool & they wouldn't take her on!"

"Our Craig! Will you stop winding grandad up!!"

"They've had to look further afield since the Bosman Ruling."

"You're quite wrong officer, we were not evading arrest by jumping out of a second floor window and running 200 metres across a barb-wire strewn railway siding. We were merely practicing for 'Gladiators'."

"Am I on free dinners?" "Nope. Just the one."

READY ~ STEADY...
GO!
NO, SORRY ~ ONLY KIDDING!
GRAND NATIONAL
STARTER'S OFFICE

"*I wonder . . . do London kids watch 'Brookside'?*"

"They're politically very correct here aren't they."

"Keep your eye on him.
He picks his nose in class when he thinks nobody's looking . . ."

"Slipped a couple of places since we were last here . . ."

"*I am NOT an illegal street trader.
I give the stuff away and people give me money 'cos they like me.*"

*"Let him get on with it Mr. Armitage -
We've obviously made a breakthrough!"*

"Genuine? Course it's genuine!"

"Not too many of those around here . . ."

"This is Terry - my cash flow manager . . ."

"Bloke from 'Cream' says he'd rather we didn't use that name."